AIM FOR THE SKIES

JERRIE MOCK and JOAN MERRIAM SMITH'S
Race to Complete AMELIA EARHART'S Quest

By AIMÉE BISSONETTE • Illustrated by DORIS ETTLINGER

Jerrie Mock took her first airplane ride when she was seven years old. The rumbling of the engines filled her ears as the plane sped down the runway.

"I'm going to be a pilot," Jerrie announced when the plane landed.

At first, Jerrie dreamed of flying across her home state of Ohio. But years later, when she hurried home from school to listen to radio broadcasts about Amelia Earhart, Jerrie decided Ohio wasn't big enough.

I want to do what Amelia is doing, Jerrie thought. *I want to see the whole world.*

Joan Merriam's first plane ride was in 1952, when she was fifteen years old. During the flight, the pilots invited her into the cockpit.

When they landed, Joan told her mother she wanted to learn how to fly a plane. She started flying lessons and got her pilot's license before she could even drive a car.

Joan also dreamed of flying around the world. Amelia Earhart was her idol, and Joan wanted to circle the globe following the exact route Amelia had charted. By age twenty-three, Joan was flying planes for a living. In November of 1963, she finally had enough money to buy her own plane.

It's time, Joan thought.

Back in Ohio, Jerrie felt it was time too. By then, she was married with three children. She was thirty-seven years old. She and her husband, Russ, even had their own plane and business. And Jerrie still had her dream.

One night, while she was doing dishes, Jerrie told Russ she was bored.

"Maybe you should get in your plane and fly around the world," Russ joked.

"All right," Jerrie said. "I will."

Jerrie and Joan planned for months.

They studied weather reports.

They drew up flight plans.

Jerrie sent cablegrams to far-off countries asking for permission to land at their airports.

Joan made charts and laid them the length of her living room.

Jerrie didn't know about Joan. Joan didn't know about Jerrie.

But then, several weeks before Jerrie and Joan planned to take off, the news broke. Two women had decided to fly around the world at the exact same time.

Jerrie couldn't believe it.

Joan was stunned.

Flying around the world was going to be hard enough. Now it was a race!

Jerrie and Joan scrambled to get ready.

On March 17, 1964, Joan held her breath as she sped down the runway and into the sky over Oakland, California. The extra seats in her plane had been taken out to make room for big, bulky fuel tanks. Joan had a toy koala bear stuck to a side window and a toy polar bear at her side. They would be her companions for the next several weeks.

This is for you, Amelia, she thought.

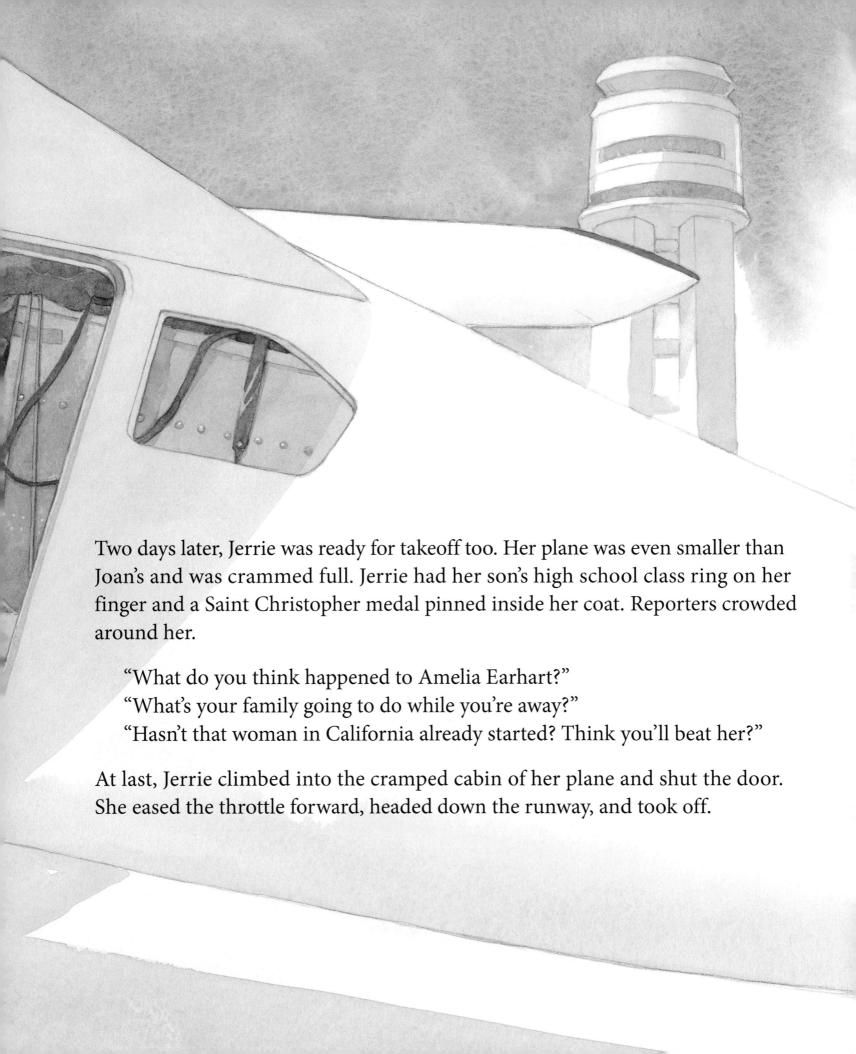

Two days later, Jerrie was ready for takeoff too. Her plane was even smaller than Joan's and was crammed full. Jerrie had her son's high school class ring on her finger and a Saint Christopher medal pinned inside her coat. Reporters crowded around her.

"What do you think happened to Amelia Earhart?"
"What's your family going to do while you're away?"
"Hasn't that woman in California already started? Think you'll beat her?"

At last, Jerrie climbed into the cramped cabin of her plane and shut the door. She eased the throttle forward, headed down the runway, and took off.

Jerrie's troubles started the first day of her flight. The long-range radio she had just installed didn't work. She had to fly over the ocean through the dangerous Bermuda Triangle with no radio communication at all. Then bad weather hit Bermuda, grounding Jerrie for six days. Jerrie grew nervous as the days dragged on. Where was Joan?

Joan's trip started smoothly. She flew from Miami to Puerto Rico and then on to Surinam in South America. As she got ready to leave Surinam, though, Joan saw gasoline leaking from her plane. There was a crack in one of her gas tanks! Joan was stuck for a week, waiting for the tank to be repaired. Where was Jerrie?

Jerrie left Bermuda and flew on. She flew to the Azores, to Casablanca, then on to Algeria, Libya, Egypt, and Saudi Arabia. Each day, it seemed, something went wrong. She battled dangerous ice buildup, burning radio wires, and bad weather. She flew into a sandstorm over the Arabian Desert and couldn't see. Everything around her lost its shape and became blurry.

Don't panic, Jerrie thought. *Use the instruments. Stay on course.*

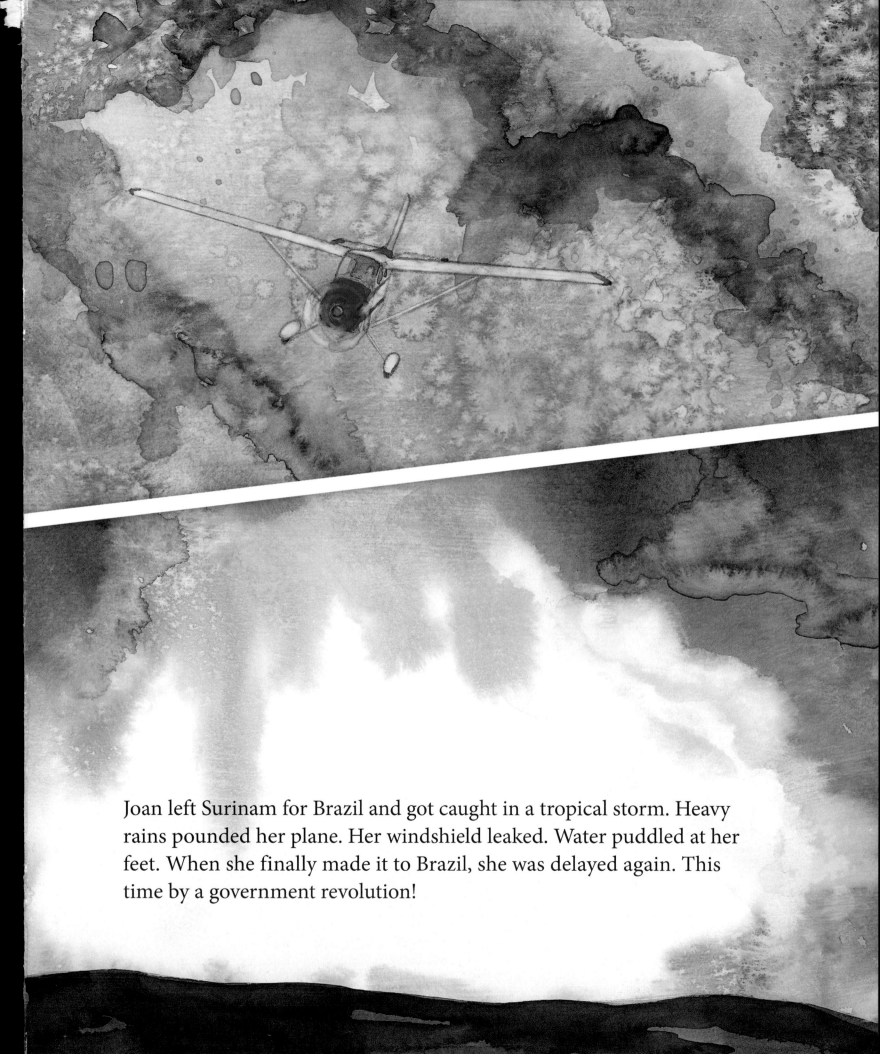

Joan left Surinam for Brazil and got caught in a tropical storm. Heavy rains pounded her plane. Her windshield leaked. Water puddled at her feet. When she finally made it to Brazil, she was delayed again. This time by a government revolution!

On and on Jerrie and Joan flew, day after day, week after week.

Jerrie's engine overheated and started burning fuel on the way to the Philippines. She had to kill her engine mid-flight to switch fuel tanks—a risky move she had practiced only once over Kansas when she had the help of a copilot.

Joan flew through terrible heat over Africa that made her groggy and weak. She had to splash water on her face to stay alert. Then she hit severe turbulence. It took all of Joan's strength to keep her plane from veering off course.

Jerrie and Joan pushed each other.
Neither wanted to lose.

Russ told Jerrie in his telegrams
and phone calls that she needed to
fly faster…. Joan was winning.

And when Joan arrived in Pakistan, people told her that Jerrie Mock had been there—five days ago!

On April 17, after twenty-nine days of flying, Jerrie returned to Columbus, Ohio. A huge crowd of people gathered to see her land. Flashbulbs popped and everyone cheered when she touched down. Russ ran to her with their daughter, Valerie, in his arms.

Jerrie's heart pounded. She had done it. She had flown around the world. She had won the race.

Joan was in Lae, New Guinea—the last place Amelia Earhart was seen alive—when she heard the race was over. She knew she had been falling behind, but the news was still hard to take.

Joan sent Jerrie a telegram and left for Guam:

Sincere congratulations on your great achievement. Hoping the clear skies and tailwinds of your trip will always be with you.

When she got to Guam, she took a long walk.

As Joan walked, she thought. She thought about her childhood dream. She thought about the race and she thought about losing.

Then Joan thought about Amelia Earhart. Honoring Amelia was what Joan had wanted to do all along, wasn't it? Jerrie had won the race. But did that make Joan a loser? No. Joan could still do what she set out to do.

I'll finish.

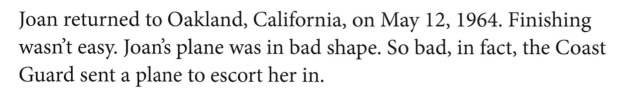

Joan returned to Oakland, California, on May 12, 1964. Finishing wasn't easy. Joan's plane was in bad shape. So bad, in fact, the Coast Guard sent a plane to escort her in.

When Joan landed, she was greeted by a cheering crowd. A large banner stretched across the terminal. It read, WELCOME HOME, JOAN! *OUR* AMELIA EARHART.

Joan's eyes filled with tears.

The race had been unexpected. In the end, though, both women had fulfilled their dreams.

Jerrie had visited countries she had only dreamed of as a girl. She had pushed herself to her physical limits and became the first woman to fly around the world.

Joan honored Amelia, just as she'd said she would. She circled the globe, following Amelia's exact route along the equator. No other pilot—man or woman—had flown that distance alone.

And both received telegrams from Amelia Earhart's sister, Muriel Earhart Morrissey, who congratulated them and thanked them for honoring Amelia— a pilot who, like them, chose to follow her dreams.

Author's Note

Although it made for exciting news, it is a shame that Jerrie and Joan took off for their around-the-world flights at the same time. Calling it a race sold their accomplishments short. It made it easy to overlook the differences in their routes and in the planes they flew. Jerrie's eleven-year-old Cessna was a single-engine plane, which some thought put her at greater risk over long ocean crossings. Joan's twin-engine Piper Apache was faster, but her route was nearly five thousand miles longer and more prone to bad weather.

Press coverage also sold their accomplishments short. Reporters called Jerrie and Joan "flying housewives." They commented on their hairstyles and their husbands. One reporter even wrote that the life vest Jerrie wore when flying over open water spoiled her outfit of "a white blouse, blue skirt, and matching handbag."

Jerrie and Joan were experienced pilots. Each set speed and distance records even before they attempted their around-the-world flights. They skillfully handled midair emergencies and mechanical problems, as well as "red tape" on the ground. They had to rely on their own judgment. No one was there to assist them.

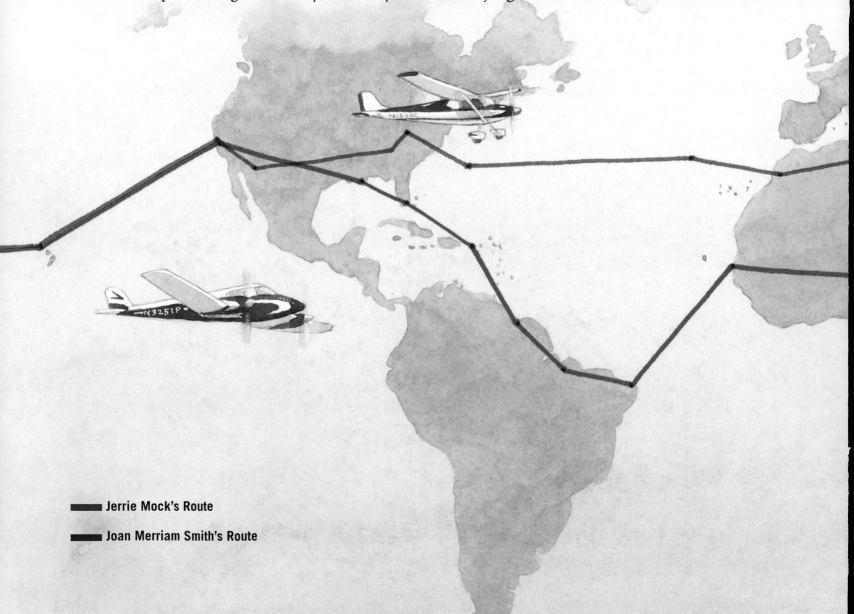

━━━ Jerrie Mock's Route

━━━ Joan Merriam Smith's Route

In 1965, Joan died in a plane crash in California's San Gabriel Mountains. She was twenty-eight years old. At the time, she was planning a first-time polar flight.

Jerrie was eighty-eight years old when she died in 2014. She lived to see the fiftieth anniversary of her successful flight and the unveiling of a statue in her honor at Port Columbus International Airport in Columbus, Ohio. Jerrie's plane, the *Spirit of Columbus*, is now part of the Smithsonian's National Air and Space Museum collection.

Want to learn more about Jerrie and Joan? Read more!

Merriam, Joan. "I Flew Around the World Alone." *The Saturday Evening Post* [237, no. 27] (July 25, 1964): 77-83.

Mock, Jerrie. *Three-Eight Charlie*. Second Ed. Self-published, Granville, OH: Phoenix Graphix Publishing Services, 2013.

Phillips, Taylor. *Racing to Greet the Sun: Jerrie Mock and Joan Merriam Smith Duel to Become the First Woman to Fly Solo Around the World*. Self-published, Around the Writer's Table, 2015. Kindle.

Pimm, Nancy Roe. *The Jerrie Mock Story: The First Woman to Fly Solo Around the World*. Athens, OH: Ohio University Press, 2016.

Saunders, Amy K. "The Long, Lonely Flight of Jerrie Mock: How an Ohio Housewife Flew Around the World, Made History, and Was Then Forgotten." BuzzfeedNews, April 12, 2014. https://www.buzzfeed.com/amyksaunders/the-untold-story-of-the-first-woman-to-fly-around-the-world?utm_term=.bqRpw7vXy#.nvvOD6MNG

Disclaimer: Above website information (including link) was accessible and correct as of the publication date of this book.

All my love to Bryan, Maureen, and Aliza—and to my parents,
Bev and Clem, who taught me to believe the sky's the limit.

—Aimée

✢

For Geraldine "Jerrie" Mock and Joan Merriam Smith

—Doris

Cessna is a trademark of Cessna Aircraft Company.

Piper Apache was designed and built by Piper Aircraft, Inc.

Sleeping Bear Press®
2395 South Huron Parkway, Suite 200
Ann Arbor, MI 48104
www.sleepingbearpress.com

Printed and bound in the United States.

10 9 8 7 6 5 4 3 2 1

Library of Congress Cataloging-in-Publication Data

Names: Bissonette, Aimée M., author. | Ettlinger, Doris, illustrator.
Title: Aim for the skies : Jerrie Mock and Joan Merriam Smith's race to
complete Amelia Earhart's quest / written by Aimée Bissonette ;
illustrated by Doris Ettlinger.
Description: Ann Arbor, MI : Sleeping Bear Press, [2018] | Audience: Age 6-10.
Identifiers: LCCN 2018006625 | ISBN 9781585363810
Subjects: LCSH: Aeronautics—Competitions—Juvenile literature. | Flights
around the world—Juvenile literature. | Mock, Jerrie, 1925-2014—Juvenile
literature. | Smith, Joan Merriam, 1936-1965—Juvenile literature. |
Earhart, Amelia, 1897-1937—Juvenile literature. | Women air
pilots—United States—Biography—Juvenile literature. |
Aeronautics—Records—Juvenile literature.
Classification: LCC TL537 .B57 2018 | DDC 629.13092/520973—dc23
LC record available at https://lccn.loc.gov/2018006625